FIVE GOOD REASONS TO LIVE

GREG PEARCE

· AND 5 MORE ·

Ark House Press
arkhousepress.com

Cataloguing in Publication Data:
Title: Five Good Reasons to Live
ISBN: 978-0-6455947-8-2 (pbk.)
Subjects: Christian Resource.

Layout by initiateagency.com
Illustrations by Pauline Overbeeke
Cover photo Peter Fraser
Assistance with text Claudia Proeve

CONTENTS

LOOKING FOR MEANING

"Thirteen billion light years," said President Biden. "Thirteen *billion!*" He sounded dumbfounded, and he meant to. He was responding to the first pictures from the James Webb Space Telescope.

A universe so impossibly huge that its distance is measured in time! As long as my life takes me

to live it, it is a mere cough in time. My planet, even my entire galaxy, a mere pinpoint in space. What significance can my one little life have?

I was in year seven when I first asked that question. We had got our *Readers' Digest Great World Atlas*. Our galaxy was one of billions, unimaginably old.

At bedtime we put the book down. "We don't mean nothin'," my brother said, and I thought the same. Are we just flesh and innards that can talk? Has no one made us? Could we know it if someone had? I thought my life meant nothing at all.

LIVING WITHOUT MEANING

Since then I've read the writings of unbelievers. For them life came from no one and has no meaning. One called the whole universe "a fortuitous concourse of atoms", a product of pure chance and nothing else.

But the problem I have found is that they can't live true to their belief. They can't live as though life has no meaning. Most atheists or agnostics live very meaningfully. Bertrand Russell led the campaign for nuclear disarmament. Richard Dawkins, really pushed to say what the meaning of life was, replied, "Well, er, do as you would be done by, I suppose." Other unbelievers paint pictures or give lectures as though the world is brim full of meaning.

So I found it impossible to stay believing in nothing: you just couldn't live that way.

ONE PLACE TO LOOK

I was raised in a church-going family, so I turned back to the Christian faith to see what it had to offer. What I found is that there is an immense mystery, for sure, hidden for ages. But it's not remained hidden.

"No one has ever seen God," says John's Gospel. Everyone agrees with that point, believer and unbeliever. Then it goes on, "It is God the only Son, who is close to the Father's heart, who has made him known."

That's the claim to check out. On it hangs this: if it's true, then we come from one who is personal, more personal than ourselves. God is then someone we can actually relate to. And that would be why it's quite impossible for most of us to be happy with thinking ourselves nothing but lumps of carbon product. We can't stop being who we really are.

WHY JESUS?

Jesus' claim to reveal God is, of course, immensely important. It's the greatest news ever if it's true. It's preposterous if it's not. It is nothing less than the promise that he can give us the real meaning of our lives.

You can easily read about Jesus. The Gospels give you plenty that he said and did. You need to get to know the real person for yourself, or anything I say is unlikely to convince you that he's for real.

J.B. Phillips was already a minister when he translated the New Testament "for the people of today." So he had to look really closely at Jesus. It was as though he saw Jesus for the first time. The minister became a believer. He called his book about the experience "Ring of Truth". Jesus proved himself.

It's like that in relationships: as you get to know

people you decide who you can really trust. They prove themselves, or they don't. Certainly not everyone who met Jesus was convinced of him. He was, after all, crucified by deadly enemies.

But for those who believe in him, he is not just one of the things we believe along with everything else. Rather, he gives us the true significance of life itself.

"Whoever has seen me has seen the Father," he said.

So what meaning can my life have? This cough in time, this pinpoint in space, is known and cherished and addressed by the One who made it all. I'm called God's dear one.

AS EASY AS THAT?

To believe in Jesus rocks you to your boots, because it means saying every other theory and all the other values you thought were so important aren't really at all. At least, not centrally important, like this truth. I don't know anyone who has truly trusted Jesus who hasn't experienced some crisis in the process. It's like giving up your old ideas as false gods, or idols, when you've been very attached to them.

Jesus never hid it from anyone that putting him first threatens us. One time many of his followers left him. "What about you?" he said to those who remained. "Will you leave too?"

Their spokesman Peter said, "Lord, who else can we go to? You have the words of eternal life."

THE CASE OF KATE MCSKIMMING

Life was happening as planned. The usual highs and lows.

I grew up in the '60s, my father a hard working salesman, with an even harder working stay-at-home mother to me and my seven brothers and sisters. My family was the centre of my world. I was taught to share, to stick up for myself, to care for others, be honest, truthful, resourceful, and to know the value of a dollar. Love and belonging created a binding force in my life.

For the final four years of secondary school I headed to an Anglican girls' school. Regular chapel services were mandatory. My parents took me to church and Sunday school for a while and occasionally I'd decide to walk there of a Sunday on my own. We said grace before our evening meal, but that was more a habit than a prayer. It was an indication that we could start the meal. My family were never particularly religious but we were encouraged to know Bible stories and to be aware of the major tenets of the Bible and to lead a good life.

I became a teacher and married Ian. Ian's

parents were quite forcefully religious, so that he shunned religious routines despite his lingering faith in God. We had two great children and were both working in good jobs and running our own business. We had bought and renovated a couple of old houses, been on holidays overseas and followed our own dreams.

We'd just sold our hobby farm, realising that our tree change dream was going to be too much hard work, and had bought another 'renovator's delight' turn-of-the-century home in Aldgate. Things had been a bit stressful with shifting ideas, but nothing we weren't able to cope with.

Then, out of nowhere, bam! The world I was so sure of was changed forever. I couldn't fathom what it all meant. Images that will stay in my memory forever.

I went to bed early that night. Ian sat up watching TV. It happened. He was stunned and horrified. I didn't see or hear anything until the next morning. He quietly told me as I woke.

I remember him saying, "Last night I saw something I hope I never have to see again. I thought it was a trailer for a horror movie."

But see it again we did; over and over and over

again. Aeroplanes full of people being flown into skyscrapers full of people! The horror we could only imagine in a movie was really happening. The vision of people scrambling to rooftops, running from dust clouds, smoke and fire, jumping. Messages from captives in buildings and on board planes. Horror. Terror. The world was never going to be the same.

I checked my family. My heart went to the victims, my thoughts to the impact. That day felt eerie. I was shaken to my core. All security and peace seemed under attack by such evil.

It took a while for me to come to the knowledge that such evil would not rule, nor win. There was something even stronger. Hope was not lost.

I knew I had to reconnect for real with that hope in order to give this life meaning. To find what it is that gives this life purpose and direction, hope, security and, most importantly, love.

It was because of the atrocity of September 11, 2001, that I sought the opposite of it, and I again found hope. Through listening to others of faith, conversing with Jesus in prayer, the wonder of creation revealing itself to me and noticing 'God moments' big and small, I came to realise that I have always been blessed and guided by Jesus. He has always been with me, loving me, even though I'd been going it alone. I didn't have to any more. I opened my heart to Jesus once again. Jesus was the answer, the reassurance, love and omnipresent friend I was seeking. Jesus reclaimed me and gave my life new meaning, love and hope for the future, in eternity with him. Because Jesus took upon himself the sins of the world, including mine, and in return gave me eternal life with him as Lord God, I rediscovered that peace, security and assurance of love and hope while here on Earth. Since then I've grown, learned more and lived more meaningfully and purposefully than ever before. I read. I pray. I share with others. I know Jesus and talk with him everyday. I know Him as love and hope. What could be more meaningful as a reason for life?

FORGIVENESS

Not everyone feels the need for forgiveness. For some, life owes them the apology. What has happened to them is everyone else's fault. I've not found that thinking like that ever sets anyone free at all, but knowing God's forgiveness does, fully.

I once preached in a little town in the US, in South Illinois. The local Rotary Club took me on a visit to the Marion Federal Penitentiary, the prison for the country's most extreme criminals — like, they'd murdered in prison. At the solitary confinement cells my heart pounded. What would I do when I saw a prisoner there? Well, not two metres away a prisoner locked me in his gaze. He leered at me. My response? I looked away!

To this day I regret that. I wish I'd said, "G'day, mate." Because I knew something about him that I'm sure he didn't know about himself. I knew that God made him. His life was precious. Jesus had died for him. In doing that Jesus had taken full responsibility for all the mess this man had made of his life, and taken it to its conclusion, such a separation from God and from who God had made him to be that the conclusion was death itself. Jesus had died that death.

So if he knew Jesus he could know complete forgiveness. He need not waste his time on any excuses at all, any blame he wanted to put on others.

WHO NEEDS IT MORE?

He and I would be in the same boat. With my quite respectable up-bringing, I was no less a sinner than he was. That is because our only true sin is the one we all share. There's only one real sin. It's putting our trust somewhere else than in God.

In fact Jesus was clear about this point: religious people are at bigger risk than others here because they're so tempted to put their trust in themselves — they think they're good. So everyone, but everyone, needs forgiveness before God. Jesus shows it, and Jesus gives it.

HOW GOOD IS THAT?

If you go to church you may hear the leader say, after you have confessed your sins, "Your sins are forgiven." It's said so often that you'd think church-goers were the happiest, most care-free people on the planet. It's not always so.

One week I was to speak about forgiveness. What could I say that they didn't know already?

I asked three volunteers: "How forgiven are you?"

One said, "Well, I try. I try to do the right thing."

The next said, "Well, I do my best. I try not to do too much wrong."

The third said, "I'm fully forgiven."

Then I said, "Tell me, how big a sinner are you?"

The first said the same as before: "I try. I really try to do the right thing."

The second said, "Well, I'm not a criminal or anything. I don't do murder and that sort of thing."

The third, the one who was fully forgiven, said, "I'm totally a sinner."

There you have it: the one who cheerfully said she was a sinner, a total sinner, also cheerfully knew that she was fully forgiven.

Guess who was keenest to tell others about Jesus?

Her good news wasn't: "Hey, guys! I have good news for you! We must all try harder!" (Who would ever want to tell anyone that?)

Instead her good news was, "Hey, guys, we're not stuck with what we have made of our lives. We're not victims of our past. Our past no longer

has to control us. God's forgiveness is total. He's given us a future."

I think, as far as our real characters go, and our emotional health, our sickness comes from our past; our health comes from our future. That's why I find forgiveness through Jesus, and why I find it sets me free for life, the best it can be.

AS EASY AS THAT?

It sounds simple: Jesus has paid up for us. God commits to forgive us and set us free.

Again, however, I don't know anyone who has found God's forgiveness who hasn't had some personal crisis about it. Picture yourself getting down on your knees and saying to God, "I'm sorry. I've been trusting myself. Now I need to trust you alone, and I thank you that when Jesus died for common sinners He died for me." To say this exposes our most resistant point, our pride. That has to go. It's the hardest thing in the world for some of us — until we do it!

THE CASE OF RAE

Rae is now happily married. But when she was a

telephonist in the 1960's, away from her family, she fell pregnant through a fleeting relationship. It was the time when you did not usually keep the child.

Offered a place in a home for unwed mothers, Rae went interstate, to Geelong. Instead of entering the home, she found her way to live for nine years as a helper for a single mother of six children. The woman proved to be a most chaotic person with multiple personalities and no idea of budgeting. She fell pregnant yet again, this time to her priest. Despite all this chaos, Rae was able to stay with her and to keep and love her own child.

She was determined that she would not let her child down, but she did feel that she had let God down.

Her father died. Her mother suffered a stroke and was cared for by Rae's sister. And Rae was interstate feeling totally alone.

Then her sister wrote. It was springtime in the Adelaide Hills, and Rae was even more alone.

She found herself praying in a park in Torquay, "Lord, I've reached the end. I can't keep going."

She saw a grey tunnel with no light. There was no positive future for her child.

She heard a voice cut through her sobbing: "Rae, I did not tell you to be here. You can go home."

Things fell into place. Her mother provided a home. One morning, after the years of living hand to mouth, bills unpaid, living by candle light when the power was cut off, Rae found herself putting out the bin and thinking, "This is what it's like to be part of a normal community."

She prayed for a husband who would be a father to her son, who would care for her mother, and who would sometimes have to go away with his work! A fine man married her. Her mother lived with them. Her son had his own Dad: "It's meant everything to him." And, yes, he had times away with work.

She knew Christ had forgiven her everything: "I know he has."

So what did she still have to learn? After all that, it came as a surprise when her mother died. Rae was looking at the stars on a cold June night, thinking of her mother.

"I had a vision of my mother as a nineteen year old, young and happy — joyous. I saw all of this, yet I could not forgive myself. I saw such a vision of joy, yet just then all I could feel was self-pity."

It was one more thing she had to learn about forgiveness: to forgive herself. To take hold of Christ's forgiveness and to forgive herself for her ungratefulness at that joyful and precious gift.

"I am still learning. I am learning to yield to what the Lord says. I'm really made aware that when Jesus told Peter that Peter would deny him,

Jesus knew beforehand that he would. Yet he forgave him. So he knew about me beforehand, and how I would run. I feel he foresaw my sin, and he forgave me. He is concerned and interested in his children.

"The other day we were doing a crossword. I said, 'What does *exculpation* mean?' My husband looked it up. 'It means *free from blame — acquit,*' he said. That's it! That's what's happened to me!"

FINDING DIRECTION

All this energy we have been given, all this creativity: what is it for? You've possibly heard of the forlorn notice on a tombstone: "Here lies a man who was born without reason, lived without purpose and died by chance." I imagine that he is the one who asked for that to be written after his death. He must have thought he was the living disproof of my first point, that we in fact can't live without meaning because it is inbuilt.

From the moment I received Jesus into my life (I was an older teenager) if anyone asked me what my faith meant to me, the first thing I *wanted to say* was "I'm utterly forgiven!" But the thing I *did say* was the second thing: "Now," I used to say, "I have a sense of purpose."

I felt that all that energy and creativity was *for* something.

NEW TERRITORY

I have a friend, Derek, who came to a town in which I once lived, to speak about Jesus. Derek had himself lived there as an electrician before he became a Christian. One of the women who came to hear Derek told her husband that Derek was back.

"Derek?" he said. "The one who punched me out at the pub?"

"That'd be right," said Derek, when I

reminded him of it. He remembered it well.

What had changed? Derek now lived in new territory.

CROSSING A BORDER

One of the first books I read as a new Christian had this illustration. Say you're on a train from France to Germany. You cross the border. You look around. Outside, things don't look very different. But the minute you cross the border you are no longer in the old country. You are now in a new country, 100%. Just because things look the same does not mean that you are still in France! You're not even partly in France.

And as you go on in the new country this will be confirmed for you: it will look less like the French postcards, more like the German. As you go on, things take the character of the country you are now in.

When Derek acknowledged Jesus Christ as his Lord, (the manager of his life), he'd moved into a new territory. He had a new owner, really. The New Testament is as radical as that. So he got a new direction for living. Jesus was really in him, or, as he found, the Holy Spirit was in him, sent by God to make Jesus real to us. Derek was now taking on the character of the new world in which he lived.

AS EASY AS THAT?

If I tell you the kinds of things God uses to keep his relationship with us front and centre, they sound like pretty dull conventional behaviour: praying, and reading the Gospels, (and beyond them, the rest of the Bible), and worshipping with other believers.

But I have found that when you really meet God in Jesus, something much more revolutionary is going on underneath that staid exterior. God uses these things to communicate with us!

It can cause a bit of a crisis. That comes if we try to hang on to our own comfort and our own pet ambitions. God is putting us in a different field from that. It's called "the Kingdom of God"

This kingdom is not just the things we dread! It's rather that we become available for anything God wants. It's put this way in one service: "Christ has many services to be done; some are suitable to our natural inclinations and material interests, others are contrary to both."

So I have friends who have simply prayed for God's direction for their lives, and checked their thoughts with friends at church, and found themselves led all over the world doing things they'd never have dreamed of doing if it was just up to them. One launched a physiotherapy department in Afghanistan, in the midst of civil war. A Doctor in Nepal, a teacher of Sudanese refugees in Egypt, a translator in Chad, an educator in Java: God takes people from high paid positions to places of great suffering because they are re-directed by his Spirit to leave behind everything except what matters to Jesus.

Not just those heroic ones, but everyone who is allowing Jesus to have his way in their lives, can find that his character can grow in you. His passions become yours. People who follow God's promptings don't all land in the world's hot spots, as I may have implied above. Whether they teach school, fix cars or collect the pension, they deeply desire the best for others. They're good to meet when you're down on your luck. They've tasted renewal. The kingdom of God, said Jesus, is heading for "the renewal of all things".

You can find your life's direction through following Jesus. It's about the most fulfilling way you could possibly live.

THE CASE OF ROB CHRISTIE

You meet a big man with a big voice when you meet Rob Christie. He has made his living in the business of trailer and chassis equipment. But he has not always put his energy under the direction

of Jesus Christ. He used to recognise Jesus as real, but not fervently enough to go to church of a Sunday.

"I thought I could do it all myself. Now I've realised that for some purpose Jesus has patiently watched over and guarded my life until I've understood that it's his plan for me, not mine, that's important."

In 2003 he and his wife Susan thought they should go to Sunset Rock on Good Friday.

"The service blew our socks off," Rob says. "We just had to be there Easter Day."

They joined a home group where Rob, never having been able to pray aloud, learned to do so and no one laughed.

"The patient support of my home group is a real blessing and greatly cherished."

Now prayer is so important to him that he has initiated Prayers at the Rock, an open time of prayer late on Friday afternoons, where people can speak with God with great freedom in a variety of ways.

It arose from following through on what he saw in Indonesia: a room in an apartment complex devoted to prayer 24/7. People coming and going, music a part of it, led to pray as the Spirit of God leads.

Certain things have opened up for Rob and Susan since they sought to let God put things in their minds. They have been to Indonesia four times in mission teams, building structures in orphanages and training carers. "Every time I've prayed we'd have the people we need with the skill set we needed. Every time the Lord provided us with the money, or more than enough. Last time we only had five in the team, half the usual number. We still got the job done, thirty minutes before the plane took off."

They support work among Syrian women refugees. Rob is treasurer of the project. "One time we needed $3000. We had $460 twenty-four hours out. I prayed. By the time the transfer needed to happen we had the money and then some."

And he loves the relationships he has been led to form, deep relationships with men who have done it tough in prison, who have their own profound insights into the ways of God.

This life is a far sight from the way life went before he really engaged with Christ. He will speak of prayer. He will speak of reading the Bible with daily helps. He will speak of life together. But how God uses these things to direct you needs you to be expectant, tuning into God's leading, being available.

In practice it's like this: "Ideas come to me out of the blue. I haven't been thinking about them. This alerts me to think, wow, this could be from God. Affirming that it is from God comes from what follows, and from prayer. God is well aware that I need strong affirmation that the idea is from him and that he wants me to act on it."

In that sense the whole matter for the person willing to be led is quite experimental: step out in faith when God seems to lead, and see where he takes you.

LIFE SAVER

When you live around believers you often hear them say, "I don't know how I would have got through that without my faith. How do unbelievers do it?"

Of course most unbelievers also have their coping mechanisms for getting through hard times.

And it's quite misleading to think that a Christian believer would be protected from disaster. Jesus promised the opposite: his followers were to expect to find God's blessing in the middle of persecution, bad-mouthing, lies and slander, rejection by their families and torture by a hostile state.

If a person is baptised in Australia, they may be asked: "Do you repent of your sins?" "Do you turn to Jesus Christ?" "Do you commit yourself to God?"

In some churches in Nepal if a person is baptised, they may be asked: "Are you willing to lose your job because of your faith in Jesus?"

"Are you willing to lose your family?" "Are you willing to lose your life?"

What help is that?

NICE SURPRISES

What's more, when Christians pray, they don't always get what they want. When we do it still comes as a nice surprise.

One time I was praying for a woman who had asked for prayer. (She had a terrible home life.)

I laid hands on her and committed her to the love and grace of God. While I was praying for her, I had a very clear impression, like a clear thought coming from another, that I was being healed myself. I had had an unsightly rash on my face for some time. I felt the Lord saying, "I am healing *you*, Greg."

The prayer time finished and I forgot about it until well after I got home. I went to the mirror. The rash was completely gone.

It was, as I said, a nice little surprise, and I thanked God. I was sure he had done it.

So why the surprise? And why not every time?

DRUM ROLLS

Libby, a journalist, became a Christian in mid life. She reckoned that when you went to a concert the composer had this knack of throwing in a drum roll now and then, just when you were nodding off. That is how she described what I have set out above: God doesn't give us everything we ask for, but he throws in just enough drum rolls to wake us up. We speak of the coming Kingdom of God, when God wraps up all he is doing.

These surprises are signs of the Kingdom that is coming. They wake us up to God.

THE BIG SIGN

Of all the miracles in the New Testament there is one that seems to be the basis of them all. It's the last one of Jesus' life.

When Jesus died, so did the hopes of all his followers. It's not covered up in the records: they expected nothing. Jesus had gone. They were let down. Whatever life was to be, it would be without him.

Then read the accounts of Jesus' appearances after his death. Every Gospel shows his disciples utterly surprised. They'd been shattered. Now they were totally transformed. Jesus was alive again! They were ready to die. And that was not just bravado: it was because Jesus had conquered death.

AS EASY AS THAT?

Now you can see why Christians are not making it up when they say, "I don't know how I could have got through this without Jesus." It's because they have really been promised something that you can base your life on through the best of times and the worst of times. When he had defeated death, Jesus said, "I am with you always, to the end of the ages."

We don't even remember this all the time. But it's just an act of humble faith to say, in every situation, "I couldn't have done it without Jesus."

THE CASE OF BARRY LATTER

Barry Latter created several Beatles and Pink Floyd album covers, but here he tells of a much

bigger event in his life.

Several months after the end of the Second World War, much of the devastation could still be seen as my Mum approached the maternity ward in East London. Carefully cradling her unborn child, she must have been thinking, surely this was the war to end all wars. Having survived the war, losing her new baby would have been too much to bear. But that's almost what happened.

"I'm afraid he's very frail and is suffering from bronchial pneumonia," announced the doctor, shortly after my birth. "He only has about three days to live."

Seventy-six years later, I know God had other plans for my life. It started with the doctors, who probably had no idea of their part in God's plan. They used me as a guinea pig in my early years, trialling various experimental drugs on me, trying to combat the residual chronic asthma I suffered. Somehow, I continued to survive.

I recall asking, when I was quite young, "Mum, what are these voices I keep hearing in my head, telling me what to do?"

"They're your Guardian Angels, Barry," she

reassuringly replied. "They'll be with you all your life."

That sounded nice enough, but at the time I didn't really understand just how wonderful it was.

Throughout my childhood, my family and I were quite heavily involved in the local church. I would frequently attend morning and evening services, plus Sunday School in the afternoons. But my enthusiasm waned, and I slowly lost interest. Riding my bike, playing tennis, and making friends at Bexley Grammar was far more up my street.

When it came to Christianity, I had a head knowledge, for sure, but lacked a heartfelt companionship with Jesus. I needed to be born again. Many years later, now living in South Australia, sure as eggs are eggs, it happened!

One evening, while teaching Photography and Graphic Art at Regency Park, I suddenly couldn't talk properly. My breathing became restricted. I felt ill, ended the lesson, and returned home to an empty house. I collapsed on the floor, too weak to crawl to the phone. Eventually, the family returned from a concert and immediately called for an ambulance.

When the medics arrived, they were stumped. They were saying it looked like lockjaw, or possibly quinsy. Whatever it was, with a temperature of 105... this was serious!

The next morning, my wife met a pastor coming from the Stirling hospital as she arrived to see me. He asked, "Do you think Barry would let me pray for him?" When they asked me, I apparently grunted a reply which they took as a "Yes". However, it was two days later that the real miracle occurred.

The doctors remained puzzled. Nothing showed up on the various tests. The next night, around 3am, there was talk about them cutting into my throat. And that's when I ... drifted away ...

I began to see and feel many things that people speak about when they have a near death experience – very bright light, beautiful new colours never seen before, waves of warmth washing over me, and parts of my life flashing before me. God was healing me, for sure.

The next thing I remember, I sat up feeling almost normal. Just then, a night nurse came in. She was amazed to see me apparently transformed and back in the land of the living.

"Can I get you a drink?" she asked.

"I'd love a beer," was my reply. But when she returned, I was up and getting dressed!

"What are you doing?" she gasped.

"Oh, I don't need you anymore," I replied. "I have my own personal healer now!"

I knew I had had an encounter with the Holy Spirit, as did the ear nose and throat specialist who permitted me to go home. God had healed me, physically. But even more, he'd led me to see that He will always hold us fast ... that what we are is God's gift to us. I've heard some say that what we do with ourselves is our gift to God. But now I think that what we do with ourselves is still God's gift to us!

THE CENTRAL RELATIONSHIP

For some years before my father died we lived five hours away, so we did not see him so often. But when we did it was simply a matter of going home. I would ring the bell (to make sure he didn't have a heart attack) open the door, and walk in.

I could not do that at anyone else's place, only my own father's. That was the freedom I had as my father's son. You, if you were with me, could come in too. You could be in my father's house. You had access because you were with my father's son.

"Let's jump on the tractor," I could say, "and explore the whole place." Again, you could enjoy the whole farm because all that my father had was also mine to explore and to share.

For me, that is how we come into a relationship with God, and how we come to inherit all that God has to give. Jesus once said, "All things have been committed to me by my Father, and no one knows the Father except the Son and those to whom the Son chooses to reveal him."

When we believe in Jesus, we have the freedom to go where the Son has the right to go, and to receive what the Son receives from the Father.

THE CENTRE

This gets us near the heart of what the Christian faith is about, I think. It's centrally about relationship.

It came to me years ago when I was visiting Malaysia, and went to a Buddhist temple in a cave half way up a mountain. People came on their own, lit a taper, spent a moment, and went, still on their own.

I said to my host, "When do they get together?"

"They don't," she said. "This is what they do."

"Well, that's different," I thought.

One thing Christians do is get together. We always have, gathered together week by week, especially on the day of the resurrection of Jesus, the first day of the week. We're not even very good at it! That is, sometimes we make a name for ourselves for not being as loving and accepting as people expect. But for us, true life doesn't come by trying to escape from relationships. It comes by relationships being reconciled and fulfilled, with God, others, and even ourselves.

WHERE IT STARTS

The reason for this lies in who God is. You may have thought God is out of touch and lonely, being God. No such thing! God lives in the most joyful, fulfilled fellowship, a teeming life of love, a community: Father, Son and Holy Spirit giving themselves to each other in unimaginable delight!

So when you "come to Jesus", as we say, God lets you into relationship with himself. You come into a relationship with his Father in the Spirit. Jesus said, "There's joy in heaven" when we come. God throws a party!

It's from this God that all our life has come. That's why this life is immeasurably full of life, whichever way you look! Why we love cricket, or landscaping, or deep sea diving, or music, or catching up for a cuppa, sex and story-telling and travel and remembering the good times. We don't come from nothing and we're not made for nothing.

We come from One who lives more fully than any of us, and we're made for that fullness. The whole thing we have written about in this booklet is what God has done to restore us. That is, to bring us back into renewed relationship.

AS SIMPLE AS THAT?

If you have never invited Jesus into your life, in one way, it is very simple, because it is what we were made for all along. It flows freely from God's great love. We are actually complicating our lives if we resist God.

On the other hand, it's not just a casual thing. It will be life-changing.

It starts with a prayer like this:

Dear Father,
I believe you have made me to know you.
Thank you for Jesus, who makes you known.
I am truly sorry for living my own way.
Thank you for Jesus' death in my place,
for full forgiveness,
for restoring my relationship with you.
Thank you that Jesus is alive, risen from death,
And has promised the Holy Spirit to me.
Fill me with your Spirit,
Direct me and lead me into a growing relationship with you.
In Jesus' name, Amen.

A growing relationship with God involves praying, listening to God through getting to know your way around the Bible, and thriving together in a lively church.

Church? To be honest, I know that some struggle to trust others. Some are shy, some agoraphobic, others burnt. Joining a church scares them. But the benefits of Christian community are enormous, well worth working at.

One Anzac Day I had to march in step with the mayor and the RSL president from the RSL hall to the war memorial. I looked at those two each side of me. I was hopeless: no way could I keep in step with them. The solution? I looked ahead. I followed the drummer. Then I was in step with those each side.

If we look to Jesus ahead, in the ways I suggest above, it puts us in step with others doing the same. And that is so much more fulfilling than doing life on your own.

THE CASE OF PAULINE OVERBEEKE

Art teacher Pauline Overbeeke discovered that all relationship is reciprocal, even relationships with the things around us, and especially relationship with God. She found this in the hardest possible way.

"I did not relate to God or Jesus. Growing up, I went to Sunday school. I remember taking communion for the first time. It was just the thing to do.

"I asked my mum when we had children, 'Do you believe in God?'

"'Yes, I do.'

"But I did not know the next question.

"We were good people with a sense of propriety. I had friends who were Christians. We only went to church Christmas and Easter. They went between."

Fresh out of college as a teacher she joined a Bible study group of fine young women in the Barossa valley. It didn't go well for her. She was freaked out when she felt she should pray aloud, and she could make nothing of the little passages they read. She soon fled the group.

She spent ten years as a young teacher, travelling and teaching in Canada and New Zealand.

On returning home she thought it was time to settle down. She did. She fell in love with and married Hans. They had two children. She enrolled them in a catholic school because she wasn't against them knowing about God. In fact she approached the Orley Avenue Church in Stirling and offered to teach Sunday school (after all, she was a teacher) so that her boys would know something about God.

"I got sick of it in a month, and didn't know what I was teaching. I felt like a hypocrite."

When the boys were at university they and their father were caught up in Australia's worst mass shooting at Port Arthur. It was a major trauma. Four months later, just before Pauline left for a trip to Melbourne, her son Benjamin said, "Do you believe in God, Mum?'

"I wondered what he meant. Krishna? Buddha? We had not had a conversation about God, ever."

That night, Pauline away, Ben went up the radio tower at Crafers. He fell to his death. The coroner called it misadventure.

"It was surreal. A week later I contacted Brian Zeitz, the minister at Sunset Rock. (I found later that Ben used to sit, often at sunset, with his friends on the rocks at Sunset Rock.) During a sleepless night I was writing things in the dark that I wanted for the funeral, my communion song, *O Lamb of God, I come.* I got this weird feeling there was something in the room, blue iridescent light. If I shut my eyes I couldn't get rid of it. Then I sensed a voice saying three things, 'Hans and Warren will be all right'; 'Peace, joy, love'; 'This is the Holy Spirit', in the way that things come to you: bang! I felt joy as I'd never known it. I'd known happiness. But this was joy. I felt levitated. If I was standing I'd have fallen.

"Next morning I heard a blackbird sing so beautifully, like I'd never heard before.

"I wrote a letter to the congregation before the funeral saying we had a sense of peace. I came home and looked at the trees and everything was new. I suddenly was aware of a fullness and a knowingness. I thought I was the wisest person in the world. Hans said that people would think I was having a breakdown, but I knew exactly that I wanted to get to know God.

"We had the funeral. A friend said, 'You know I've just found Jesus. What about BSF (Bible Study Fellowship) at Sunset Rock?

"I found Jesus. I couldn't see what was real

before. I tuned in and I still tune in to get to know Jesus more. But how is anyone going to believe me if I say that this is the best that ever happened?

"I could see the workings of the Triune God. The Holy Spirit (I need visuals) I could see as a constant little flame, always there, and when God says something to us — woosh! The flame blazes! Jesus is the one who sent the Spirit. He convicts me. And I picture God the Father. Jesus takes an obedient stand as the Son. He delivers us the whole message of God through the workings of the Spirit.

"Sometimes it's hard work. There are many of the old ways that cause stumbling blocks. But what I love about my journey with Jesus is that I'm justified. I'm convicted. I want to honour Jesus in action. That's Godliness. I feel I'm surrounded by Godliness."

A LAST WORD

There remains something that feels not quite right in what I have written. I have said what it is about Jesus that makes me want to tell others about him. In one way that sounds rather self-centred: he gives me meaning, forgiveness, direction, saving help and my core relationship. As though it's all for me! If so, aren't I being a bit childish, and a little like the whole Me Generation?

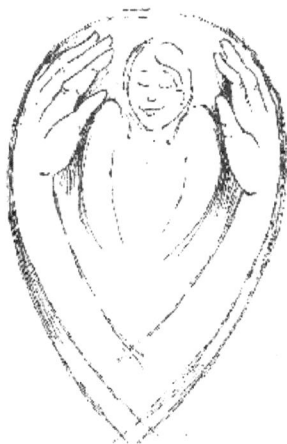

But truly, the most satisfying thing, the most maturing thing, the most authentic thing I have discovered by trusting Jesus is that I am now no longer the centre of my life at all. He is. He is at the centre of the whole universe, so has to be at the centre of my life into the bargain. Somehow, having discovered that, I feel that I've become what I am made to be. The true centre is now outside of myself. That's what we call worship. We're most truly ourselves when we forget ourselves. Then at last we're at home.